To: Charlene

SINGLE AGAIN
THE DEVOTIONAL

DALORIA MONDESIR

Be blessed always,
Daloria

Scripture quotations are taken from the King James Version unless otherwise noted.

Cover concept and design by DaLoria Mondesir

Cover Image Public Domain

SINGLE AGAIN THE DEVOTIONAL Copyright @ 2017 by DaLoria Mondesir Self-Published through CreateSpace an Amazon company.

ISBN:-10: 1977680771
ISBN-13: 978-1977680778

Printed in the United States of America

FOREWARD

There may be some line of distinction between observation and experience; a liminal state where spiritual meditation and workaday existence compete, unnoticed, by the mere mortal who finds herself confronted by life's unavoidable chaos. Most of us, myself included, are scarcely aware of the consequences of this conflict and disconnect. The Copenhagen interpretation implies (in part) that the mere act of observation changes the subject being observed. As it turns out my dear friend and church sister, DaLoria Mondesir, who has filled these pages with a searing and practical guide through human heartache, seems to be lulling us as gently as she might through the turbulence of self-doubt. She achieves this by reminding us that the physical and spiritual *should* be mindful and respectful of one another. In defense of her premise she cites authoritative sources as diverse as Holy Scripture and Leon Russell.

Indeed, much of this profoundly personal resource to the reader of faith is a celebration of the capacity of the human heart—from the depths of despair to the transcendent joy of discovering true and eternal love. Sister

Mondesir's relentless message of encouragement is based primarily in personal testimony. Her sources of inspiration are entirely supported by her research into every corner of The Bible and her own lived experience. Her references span the generations, and it results in a convincing, moving, and utile spiritual treat to those who will take the time to read, as it were, her spiritual mind.

Why DaLoria asked me to contribute this foreword is vaguely mysterious to me, though of course very flattering. While I did attend a Catholic seminary in my youth, I would scarcely qualify as a candidate to opine on the contents of a devotional this deeply considered. For even fuller disclosure, I did not complete the request in time: I always feel compelled to peruse any project on which I am to comment, and I am usually slammed by the buttresses of schedule. So, I waited to comment until after I read (today!) the publication in toto. If there is any virtue conferred to the latecomer, I hope it lies in the fact that in reading *Single Again*, the words therein came at the perfect time for me. Time and timeliness figure prominently throughout the chapters ("Isles," as our sister would have it), for example in Habakkuk 2:2-3.

Even for those who, like me, are perfectly content in wedlock, there is great wisdom and benefit here. Having been given an early viewing of *Single Again* I can say I feel advantaged over any of the powers and principalities that heretofore plagued my peace of mind. DaLoria seems to have intuited that I would, by association with her words, be something of a successful test case. I'm grateful to her (Thanks, DaLoria!—as she might say) and hopeful that your excursion through this devotional will likewise help make sense of some of the inevitable twists on the road of life. It will, I trust manifest, in your heart as a paean to be enjoyed in small doses— or through deep exploration.

Brother Harry Lennix

ENDORSEMENTS

Single Again – The devotional is insightful and easy reading. The writer's transparency affords every reader a clear picture of the trauma, emotions and pain of divorce. From the heart of an obvious overcomer DaLoria shares strategies and a bible based pathway to peace, hope and contentment.

Dr. Barbara McCoo Lewis
General Supervisor
International Department of Women
Church of God in Christ, Inc.

"A word fitly spoken is like apple of gold in pictures of silver." Proverbs 25:11

Prepare to not only admire but to be highly blessed by the words fitly spoken to you in this flagship work inspired by God an spoken through His vessel – talented author DaLoria Mondesir! These are words for our time. These are words that will enlighten and encourage you. They are brave words, thought-provoking words, challenging words. You will find yourself laughing, journaling, and celebrating God's deliverance power. The truth and wisdom that she shares will equip you to embrace the "single" and plan for a future full of God's blessings! Congratulations, DaLoria, on a phenomenal work of art! We know this is just the first of many!

Dr. Beryl A. New, Ed.D

<u>DEDICATION</u>

"And it is a good thing to receive wealth from God and the good health to enjoy it. To enjoy your work and accept your lot in life- this is indeed a gift from God. God keeps such people so busy enjoying life that they take no time to brood over the past"

Ecclesiastes 5:19 & 20 (NLT)

This Devotional is dedicated to the precious jewel that has chosen to read these pages from my heart. I give thanks and praise to my Lord and Savior Jesus Christ who has allowed me the pleasure of experiencing the promises of God and has made the Word of God alive in me. May you be challenged to persevere, encouraged to press in, and ignited to live life abundantly in the promises of God our Father.

YOU ARE ENOUGH!!!

YOU ARE LOVED!!!

MULTITUDE OF ISLES

"The Lord reigneth; let the earth rejoice; let the multitude of isles be glad therof." Psalm 97:1

These "Chapters" I have creatively renamed "Isles" as in "Islands". Sometimes when you are going through a particular season in your life, you can feel like you're an island alone…

	Introduction	Pg 1
Isle 1	It Hurts and I'm Angry!	Pg 7
Isle 2	Dealing With Rejection	Pg 11
Isle 3	Cleansing Tears and Realized Dreams	Pg 15
Isle 4	Truth and (Un)Forgiveness	Pg 20
Isle 5	Faith	Pg 28
Isle 6	Boaz Can Have a Seat!	Pg 31
Isle 7	Raise the Praise!	Pg 36
Isle 8	Entanglements	Pg 39
Isle 9	Single Doesn't Mean Alone	Pg 43
Isle 10	The Two "C's" – Coffee & Confidence!	Pg 54

Isle 11	Please Don't Kill Your Friends	Pg 58
Isle 12	The Kitchen Table	Pg 67
Isle 13	Lipstick on the Mirror	Pg 71
Isle 14	The Queen Sits	Pg 76
Isle 15	Who's in Your Ear?	Pg 80
	Final Thoughts	Pg 84
	Thank You	Pg 86
	About the Author	Pg 89
	Author's Note	Pg 90
	Contact Information	Pg 92

At some point, you have

to realize that some people

can stay in your heart

but not in your life.

-Anonymous

INTRODUCTION

"You are worthy of love – even when you make mistakes." – Sandi Krakowski

Whatever circumstances that caused you to become single again may have brought you to a place of emotional unrest, possibly questioning your worth and painfully, yet simply asking, "Why?" American singer-songwriter Bonnie Raitt touched our very souls with lyrics to her popular tune, *"I Can't Make You Love Me"*. Very true words to say the least. We may have all felt this way at some point in our lives. Trust that at some point you must transition from the "whys" to the acceptance of the reality of "what is".

As you travel through the pages of this Devotional, stop and allow yourself to feel every emotion that presents itself. Acknowledge your emotions, but don't take up residence there. Ladies, cry if you must, then get up, wash you face, "beat" your face, put on something pretty, smile at yourself in the mirror, hold your head up and keep it moving. Hopefully while reading this unique Devotional, there will be some little tidbit that will bring joy and cause you to laugh. Absorb the Word of God. Ingest it.

This Devotional was designed especially for YOU. It's not your traditional Devotional, however it does present a practical view of everyday life…and the lonely nights. You'll find that some "Isles" (chapters) are larger than others, but they all possess the same validity.

Take time for yourself. Healing will come…for some sooner, for some later…but it will come when you allow it in your heart and soul and learn to shut out the negative voices in your head. God is a healer of not just the physical, but also of the emotional as well. My prayer for YOU, firstly that if you don't know the Lord Jesus Christ as your personal savior, that you will accept Him into your heart. I pray that every woman (and man) that reads and absorbs this Devotional will allow the Lord to strengthen them with every page read. I pray that you will ***find*** *peace, laugh again, and love again.* I pray that your healing comes sooner than later, but more so you must believe that it will come.

Phenomenal Woman

Pretty women wonder where my secret lies.
I'm not cute or built to suit a fashion model's size
But when I start to tell them,
They think I'm telling lies.
I say,
It's in the reach of my arms
The span of my hips,
The stride of my step,
The curl of my lips.
I'm a woman
Phenomenally.
Phenomenal woman,
That's me.

I walk into a room
Just as cool as you please,
And to a man,
The fellows stand or
Fall down on their knees.
Then they swarm around me,
A hive of honey bees.
I say,
It's the fire in my eyes,
And the flash of my teeth,

The swing in my waist,
And the joy in my feet.
I'm a woman
Phenomenally.
Phenomenal woman,
That's me.

Men themselves have wondered
What they see in me.
They try so much
But they can't touch
My inner mystery.
When I try to show them
They say they still can't see.
I say,
It's in the arch of my back,
The sun of my smile,
The ride of my breasts,
The grace of my style.
I'm a woman

Phenomenally.
Phenomenal woman,
That's me.

Now you understand
Just why my head's not bowed.
I don't shout or jump about
Or have to talk real loud.
When you see me passing
It ought to make you proud.
I say,
It's in the click of my heels,
The bend of my hair,
the palm of my hand,
The need of my care,
'Cause I'm a woman
Phenomenally.
Phenomenal woman,
That's me.

-Maya Angelou

ISLE 1
IT HURTS AND I'M ANGRY!

"In his kindness God called you to share in his eternal glory by means of Christ Jesus. So after you have suffered a little while, he will restore, support, and strengthen you, and he will place you on a firm foundation." I Peter 5:10 (NLT)

"Be not hasty in thy spirit to be angry: for anger resteth in the bosom of fools." Ecclesiastes 7:9

"It is better to dwell in the wilderness, than with a contentious and an angry woman." Proverbs 21:19

"Be ye angry, and sin not: let not the sun go down upon your wrath:" Ephesians 4:26

Ms. Angelou told us in the most eloquent of ways, and yet in all bluntness…

"When someone shows you who they are, believe them the first time." -Maya Angelou

…but did we listen? Ms. Angelou in 12 simple words gave us a profound, and powerful instruction for relationships and life. Had most of us listened to the seasoned "Maya's" that were in our lives, well, dare I say it? We wouldn't be at the place that some of us seemingly detest dwelling in right now…but it doesn't have to persist…some things, some people and some past relationships and some old situations, you will eventually learn that the door was closed for a reason and that you should simply……leave well enough alone.

If you are determined to move from a place of hurt and anger, time and space (from the person that hurt you), prayer, commitment and faithfulness to God will become your constant companions of choice. Please take care in not allowing yourself to become bitter and angry. Ecclesiastes 7:9 reminds us; *"Do not be eager in your heart to be angry, For anger dwells in the heart of fools."*

I understand that anger may take hold to some degree because we are human. And in some cases, not only do you have the right to be angry, but it's almost to be expected. Not to be redundant, but rather to encourage you, for your own sake, please don't remain there. Begin to elevate your mind, heart and spirit through the anointed passages of scripture. Become acquainted with those verses that will assist and strengthen you to make it through…be encouraged, you will make it through. Don't just read, but you must meditate on and believe the Word of God. Spend quality time in prayer pouring out your heart to God, He hears and He will deliver you and heal you where you hurt.

(7) "And the peace of God, which passeth all understanding, shall keep your hearts and minds through Christ Jesus." (8) "Finally, brethren, whatsoever things are true, whatsoever things are honest, whatsoever things are just, whatsoever things are pure, whatsoever things are lovely, whatsoever things are of good report; if there be any virtue, and if there be any praise, think on these things."
Philippians 4:7-8

"Thou wilt keep him in perfect peace, whose mind is

stayed on thee: because he trusteth in thee."
Isaiah 26:3

There are so many scriptures throughout the Word of God that will comfort your grieving heart. Healing is available to your broken heart…if you will but accept it.

ISLE 2
DEALING WITH REJECTION

(17) "The righteous cry, and the Lord heareth, and delivereth them out of all their troubles." (18) "The Lord is nigh unto them that are of a broken heart; and saveth such as be of a contrite spirit." (19) "Many are the afflictions of the righteous: but the Lord delivereth him out of them all. (20) "He keepeth all his bones: not one of them is broken."
Psalms 34:17-20

"Finally, bretheren, whatsoever things are true, whatsoever things are honest, whatsoever things are just, whatsoever things are pure, whatsoever things are lovely, whatsoever things are of good report; if there be any virtue, and if there be any praise, think on these things."
Philippians 4:8
"Sometimes when things fall apart, they may actually be falling into place."
-J. Lynn, Fall with Me

"Rejection is a divine announcement that those persons can no longer prosper you. It means that it's time for

11

*you to move on, but you didn't move on quick enough
from that relationship, so they rejected you. Rejection
is not a sign of inferiority, it is a sign for you to move
on. It means that the relationship or person no longer
has the capacity to support your purpose and your
destiny. You don't cry because someone rejects you,
you give yourself a going away party!"*
– Dr. Cindy Trimm

Oddly enough, when I began to think about
the "Isle" of Rejection, the very first thought
that came to my mind was, "The Final
Frontier". Not to get too "Star Trekish", but
rejection can seem like you've entered a land
of no return. Just seemingly no way out of
these excruciatingly painful emotions. That
this (unhappy) single state will be yours
forever. Well, that's exactly what the enemy
wants you to believe. He wants you to believe
that this failed love was the last of the last,
and that you will never experience that real,
solid, captivating, committed love. Well, I just
happen to believe God, and I believe what He
said in His Word is true, and I stand on it.
Psalms 37:4 states, *"Delight thyself also in the
Lord; and he shall give thee the desires of thine heart."*
If your true desire is to be in a committed,
stable, lasting and loving marital relationship,

then you must believe God for it. It's an act of faith.

At the time that I'm writing this particular Isle, I am *Single Again* – not dating anyone, and with no current marriage prospects. However I am productive, happy, and whole. I'm far from perfect, but am I'm constantly working on myself to become a better 'me'. I try not to be too hard on myself. I'm not constantly focused on being married or being in a relationship. I don't look at every man that shows interest in me as a potential husband. Some guys are just friends, and that's fine. Every girl needs a guy friend to hang out with. And even though this current *Single Again* state wasn't planned, the reality of it is that it is here. Now that it is here, I've embraced where I currently am. And although it's been a painful journey, I am now at peace with it.

"And the peace of God, which passeth all understanding, shall keep your hearts and minds through Christ Jesus." Philippians 4:7

Examine your heart. Focus on the Lord. Work on you and let God do the rest....just relax, it's going to be okay. (Thanks, Pastor Jeff!)

Note: This is probably the absolute best time for you to journal. This is where you can pour out all of the pain and anguish on the pages of your *Single Again Journal*. If you really need to 'let it out' and don't want to ever read that particular entry ever again, then grab some loose leaf notebook paper and go for it! Empty yourself of whatever negativity you're currently feeling. Now, after you've done that, find an old foil pie tin and go outside and burn it! As the paper burns, allow all of those hurtful feelings to burn away as well.

ISLE 3
CLEANSING TEARS AND REALIZED DREAMS

"Tears are prayers too, they travel to God when we can't speak"
(Reference to Psalms 56:8)

"You keep track of all my sorrows. You have collected all my tears in your bottle. You have recorded each one in your book."
Psalms 56:8 (NLT)

"The sacrifices of God are a broken spirit: a broken and a contrite heart, O God, thou wilt not despise."
Psalms 51:17

I should have purchased stock in Kleenex©!! Oh yes, the tears will undoubtedly come – as they should. Tears can actually be very cleansing, but please don't allow yourself to cry continuously. As thoughts of failed relationships and a life not lived swirl through your mind and emotions, sometimes you can't help but cry. It's okay. The times of crying especially when you know that the Lord is bottling every tear can be very healing. I believe that tears can also be prayers. The Lord interprets our tears and He knows what they mean. Sometimes in prayer, the words don't always come. Just be still and rest in His presence, cry in the arms of the Lord and receive the comfort from Holy Spirit.

Dr. William H. Frey II, PhD has stated, *"Crying is not only a human response to sorrow and frustration, it's a healthy one."* I'm sure you know that crying is a way reduce emotional stress. Researchers tell us that if you don't have a way to release your emotions, it can cause negative physical effects on the body. I do feel however, that there is a difference between releasing one's emotions, as opposed to allowing oneself to slip into a deep depression. Painful thoughts of past broken relationships, unpleasant circumstances and sometimes unstable environments, can have the potential to cause extreme emotional distress.

In a lot of cases, you may be starting all over again. You must remind yourself that as a Christian, your steps are ordered by the Lord.

Joyce Meyer often says, *"If you got off track, don't worry, God will find you."*

I love Jeremiah 29:11; *"For I know the thoughts that I think toward you, saith the Lord, thoughts of peace, and not of evil, to give you an expected end."* I love the entire verse, but the *expected end* declaration in this verse is especially comforting. I'd like to marry this verse of scripture with Proverbs 16:3; (AMP) *"Commit your works to the Lord [submit and trust them to Him], And your plans will succeed [if you respond to His will and guidance].*

Earlier in the Introduction of this Devotional, I made mention of acknowledging your emotions but not to live there. You must find your motivation to (with the help of the Lord), pick yourself up, and begin to live and work towards the abundant life which is the believers promise.

The *'expected end'* is partially your own vision for your life based on what God says you can have.

"But thou shalt remember the Lord they God: for it is he that giveth thee ability to produce wealth, and so

confirms his covenant, which he swore to your
ancestors, as it is today."
Deuteronomy 8:18 (NIV)

"Beloved, I wish above all things that thou mayest
prosper and be in health, even as thy soul prospereth."
3 John 1:2

It's a reminder that dreams are realized through the direction of the Holy Spirit. I'm a firm believer in writing down your visions, dreams and goals and then of those visions that you are most passionate, submit them to the Lord through prayer, ask for His divine direction and then begin to *"Plan your work, and work your plan."* –Anonymous.

Read with me Habakkuk 2:2-3,
(2) *"And the Lord answered me, and said, Write the vision, make it plain upon the tables, that he may run that readeth it."* (3) *"For the vision is yet for an appointed time, but at the end it shall speak, and not lie: though it tarry, wait for it; because it will surely come, it will not tarry."*

Writing down your vision, creating vision boards, finding coaches and mentors in the relationship/ministry/business arenas who have already achieved success in your area of interest, I believe is crucial to your healing and personal growth.

You must be willing to invest in your own dreams and visions before you can expect anyone else to. Discipline, scheduling and keeping your *"Work Dream Appointments"* (quote, my own) with yourself every day is necessary. You may find that some of the things you cried about will ultimately strengthen you to minister and help someone else that is now walking the same path that you trod upon.

ISLE 4
TRUTH AND (UN)FORGIVENESS

"The Lord will perfect that which concerns me; Your mercy, O Lord, endures forever; Do not forsake the works of Your hands."
Psalms 138:8 (NKJV)

"Forbearing one another, forgiving one another, if any man have a quarrel against any: even as Christ forgave you, so also do ye."
Colossians 3:13

(14) *"For if ye forgive men their trespasses, your heavenly Father will also forgive you:"* (15) *But if ye forgive not men their trespasses, neither will your Father forgive your trespasses."* Matthew 6:14-15

"For the LORD is good; his mercy is everlasting; and his truth endureth to all generations."
Psalms 100:5 (NKJV)

"The weak can never forgive. Forgiveness is an

20

attribute of the strong." -Mahatma Gandhi

Let me begin by saying that forgiveness is not for the person that has offended, hurt or even crushed your spirit, but it is for you. You must forgive the offense(s) for your own health and well-being. When you harbor unforgiveness in your heart and mind, you open yourself up to illness and disease to say the least.

I did some research, quite a bit as a matter of fact, but I choose not to re-write or re-state some of the overwhelming facts that the medical community has provided the general public regarding how important it is to forgive, and how operating in unforgiveness can ultimately have negative effects on both your emotional and physical well-being. If this is an issue for you, I believe that it will have a greater impact on you if you do the work and take steps to research and investigate the subject for yourself.

You must forgive, plain and simple. Not only must you forgive the offender, but you must search your own heart and forgive yourself as well. If you are experiencing any form of guilt or shame as a result past relationships, through Christ you can find the strength to forgive them and yourself. What may amount to a monumental task for some, forgiveness for others may not be a problem....but it must be done. This is a non-negotiable.

You may say, *"Hey, I'm the one that was offended!", "Why do I have to forgive him/her?", "Why do I have to forgive myself?", "I will NEVER forgive them for the pain and anguish they put me through!", "They took me to hell and back! I refuse to forgive them!", "I want them to experience every hurt and pain they put me through!"*

You'll find no judgement from this author, but hopefully you will seriously feel my heart for you. Forgiveness often isn't easy, but it is always necessary. I would venture to say that if you choose to hold on to unforgiveness, you, unfortunately will be the one to suffer. Unforgiveness opens the nasty little door to a host of 'ugly relatives', such as bitterness, rebellion (witchcraft), vengeance and pride. Can you imagine all of that venom in one room? Lord, Jesus! That 'one room' is your heart, and unless you forgive, you will be obliged and obligated to entertain these ugly relatives for a long time.

Unforgiveness and pride go hand-in-hand. Pride is a terrible thing and one of the seven things that God hates. *"A proud look, and lying tongue, and hands that shed innocent blood,"* Proverbs 6:17.

You could possibly be expecting and waiting for a heartfelt apology from this person that will more than likely never come. You may also say, *"I'll forgive them when they apologize to me".*

Okay, time for real talk. Come on, put on your 'big girl's'.....This person more than likely has no intention of ever apologizing to you because they may not feel that they've done anything wrong. Moreover, the thought of apologizing may not have even crossed their little mind. Until they really allow God to touch their heart, and change their mind, the awaited apology is probably never going to happen.

You may not like this one either, but here's another dose of medicine. Pray for them. Yep, that's right. Go to God on their behalf. Pray that God would abundantly bless them! (You do want to be free, right?) The words of Jesus; (27) *"But I say unto you which hear, Love your enemies, do good to them which hate you, (28) Bless them that curse you, and pray for them which despitefully use you."* Luke 6:27, 28.

It frees you from living with the 'ugly relatives' (speaking of a bad personality) if you will. And don't worry, God has a way of dealing with these offenders of the heart in ways that prayerfully, you will never experience. Fulfill the conditions set forth for the believer in Christ. Psalms 23:5 states, *"Thou prepares a table before me in the presence of mine enemies: thou anointest my head with oil; my cup runneth over."*

Please, loved ones, I beg of you not to have an attitude of *"Get 'em, God"* or *"Just wait, God will handle you!"*, and then you lurk around and wait to see what bad thing befalls them. Wrong again. Guess what? You'll be the one to suffer because now you've traded places with the offender. Ouch! The book of wisdom, Proverbs 24:17, 18 tells us; (17) *"Rejoice not when thine enemy falleth, and let not thine heart be glad when he stumbleth:* (18) *Lest the Lord see it, and it displease him, and he turn away his wrath from him."*

There's so much word for this, there's no way it can be covered in just one Isle. However, I must point out a couple more scriptures. Please look at Psalms 37:1, 2; (1) *"Fret not thyself because of evildoers, neither be thou envious against the workers of iniquity. (2) For they shall be cut down like the grass, and wither as the green herb."* Also, Isaiah 54:17; *"No weapon that is formed against thee shall prosper; and every tongue that shall rise against thee in judgment thou shalt condemn. This is the heritage of the servants of the Lord, and their righteousness is of me, saith the Lord."*

So in other words, God's got this. Let Him handle it.

Not trying to give you gloom and doom, just a dose of reality. You can't live your life waiting for an apology. If you choose to wait (possibly for years) for that apology, you will just be existing, not really living….and worse yet, that person will still be controlling you. That's too much power! (Thank you, Bishop T. D. Jakes!!) Let it go, accept the truth for what it is and move on…they more than likely have already done so. Your unforgiving heart will sap your remaining joy right out of your life.

Here's an example.   Those of us with Southern roots know what 'sopping' is. For those that don't know, it's when you have some good ol' gravy or meat drippings on your plate and you take a piece of bread or biscuit and 'sop' up the gravy. The gravy and drippings represent the unique things about you. Your style, your joy, your creativity, your awesome smile, your laugh and on and on. The bread or biscuit represents the person that offended you. The bread is absorbing every good thing about you and is being consumed by an individual.   (For instance, 'That dude *looked so good* [that piece of bread], but he wasn't good for *you*!)

The bread is really something we don't need, but we eat it anyway. Sometimes because it's quick and convenient for a sandwich. It tastes good and makes us feel good for the moment….until you catch a glimpse of your backfield in motion and then you want to get to the gym and handle that dysfunction. The bread is something we should have left alone to start with. Make sense?

You must always return to the 'center' and take everything back to the Word of God. You also take your power back when you choose to do so. Search the scriptures, Jesus requires us to forgive. And if you take the Savior's advice, you'll live a much happier life.

ISLE 5
FAITH

"And we know that all things work together for good to them that love God, to them who are the called according to his purpose."
Roman 8:28

You may wonder how it will all come together….again, not to be redundant, but rather to encourage you to believe… *"And we know that all things work together for good to them that love God, to them who are the called according to his Purpose."* Romans 8:28. That seals it for me. Trust and believe that every frustration, every pain, every failure, every tear you've cried….is all working together for your good. Although Romans 8:28 isn't always referenced as a 'faith' scripture, it actually is just that.

For the believer, it takes faith to believe and know that everything is actually going to work out in your favor. You must know that what God has for YOU is for YOU!!! The Apostle Paul admonishes us in Hebrews 11:6, *"But without faith it is impossible to please him: for he that cometh to God must believe that he is, and that he is a rewarder of them that diligently seek him."* I would like to place emphasis on the last part of this verse…*he is a rewarder of them that diligently seek him.* That gives us (believers) a condition. We are clearly told that God will reward us if we diligently go after God and the things of God.

I do believe however, that when you earnestly seek the *face* of God (wanting to know Him more) and not just His hand (Lord, I need……), your heart changes from that of constantly praying for God to send you a mate, but rather that you want to please the Lord and you'll find yourself just simply wanting more of God. I love the hymn;

__TURN YOUR EYES UPON JESUS__

"O soul, are you weary and troubled?
No light in the darkness you see?
There's a light for a look at the Saviour,
And life more abundant and free!

Turn your eyes upon Jesus
Look full in His wonderful face
And the things of earth
Will grow strangely dim

In the light of His glory and grace

His Word shall not fail you – He promised;
Believe Him, and all will be well:
Then go to a world that is dying,
His perfect salvation to tell!"

-by Helen Howarth Lemmel

Just have faith, everything will be alright.

ISLE 6
BOAZ CAN HAVE A SEAT!

(1) "One day Naomi said to Ruth, 'My daughter, it's time that I found a permanent home for you, so that you will be provided for. (2) Boaz is a close relative of ours, and he's been very kind by letting you gather grain with his young women. Tonight he will be winnowing barley at the threshing floor. (3) Now do as I tell you-take a bathe and put on perfume and dress in your nicest clothes. Then go to the threshing floor, but don't let Boaz see you until he has finished eating and drinking. Be sure to notice where he lies down; then go and uncover his feet and lie down there. He will tell you what to do.' "
Ruth 3:1-3 (NLT)

Don't you get tired of women running around asking, *"God, where is my Boaz"*? I'll tell you exactly where Boaz is…with his Ruth!!! (Forgive me, I have to try to make you laugh at some point!!) But I get it, most of us are waiting to be found. But there are more good men out there beside Boaz. What about the Josephs, Davids, Moses, Abrahams and a world full of men unknown to us? God is preparing us for them, and also preparing them for us.

It's a good possibility that a lot of *Single Again* women are primarily expecting the same *type* of man (and in some cases, the same man…oops, did I just say that out loud?) to find them…sitting in church.

So we go to church. We go to work. Some of us go to school and the gym along with all of the routine places we normally go. We are told repeatedly that Ruth was found working, and some of us work our fingers to the bone! All in hopes that there is some elusive, gorgeous man somewhere watching us work and that he's going to magically appear at our place of business. That somehow this Adonis has been living his entire life preparing himself for you, and is waiting just for you, and no one else but you. *(Wait, it could happen!! LOL!)*

Forgive me, I couldn't help but be a bit

dramatic here – I purposely did it to stress the point that so many women seem to be so busy focusing on doing things that will cause them to be noticed and found by a man, instead of just focusing on enjoying life and becoming a better YOU. You're focus should always be on God first, but secondarily, focus on you.

(I will mention later in more detail in a section of this Devotional about my feeling of dating/relationship support groups, counseling, etc.)

When we don't focus on ourselves, the light seems to keep shining on what is missing in our lives...what we need to do to attract a man...what kind of women we need to become, how we need to measure up, hurry up and get it together so an elite man will find you worthy to spend time with him, etc. (Again, dramatics intended.)

I really do understand, but it would appear to me that you can spend so much time focusing on *the problem* of not being in a relationship (yours and everybody else's) that you end up missing out on the beauty of today. Enjoy your life. Be productive and confident. Most importantly, just be yourself. That's the best thing you can do.

Naomi put a little twist on *being found*. I love Naomi because she puts me in mind of my precious maternal Grandmother Mrs. Avie D. Robinson Walker, who has gone home to be with the Lord. I loved sitting in her kitchen watching her cook. As a little girl I loved how she paid attention to me and fed me love straight from her heart as she was serving me delicious food prepared by her loving hands. Her smile was infectious!!! She had so many funny little stories and songs that would just make me giggle with such delight!!!

As I grew older, I learned to cherish the talks we had. Oh, how I wish I could hear her voice right now. I recall in my young adult years prior to marriage, she said, (In her own unique vernacular) *"Baby, the Bible say that a man that findeth a wife, findeth a good thing! But sugah, you* **gots** *to be where you can be found!"* LOL!! That's what Naomi was doing with

Ruth. Positioning her to be found at the feet of Boaz and covered (claimed, protected and provided for).

Now I'm not suggesting that you pursue men, and please don't try to slip in to anyone's sleeping place and position yourself at their feet! What I am suggesting however is a position of confidence, faith and trust on the spiritual side, and on the natural side, be interesting and enjoy your life. I believe it was author, Mrs. Luci Swindoll that said, *"Don't just be interested, be interesting."*

Keep the focus on God first, and then work on you. Focus on who you are, re-learn what you like, things you like to do, places you like to go. This is your *"Do-Over"* phase (Thank you, Mrs. Honey Butler Bryant!) You're single again now so what better time to reposition yourself for success. But it begins with a belief in God, a belief in yourself and knowing that you can do *all things in Christ who has strengthened you.* (Phil 4:19) So get up girl! Dry your eyes, and just do the thing! And don't worry, have faith - he'll find you!

ISLE 7
RAISE THE PRAISE!

(Album and title song composed and recorded by Dr.
Judith Christie McAllister, President of the International
Music Department for the Church of God in Christ)

*"Enter into his gates with thanksgiving, and into his
courts with praise: be thankful unto him, and bless
his name."* Psalms 100:4

It's always been amazing to me how no matter
the circumstances, no matter the problem,
PRAISE will always bring you back to center.
Jesus is the center. When you *PRAISE*, you
take the focus off of yourself and your
problems and bring it back to where it
belongs. *PRAISE* is an act of
surrender…when you raise your hands in
worship to the Lord, you are demonstrating
surrender to your own will, in exchange for
God's divine will.

I must mention here however that *PRAISE*
and worship is a lifestyle, it's not your

emotions. If your *PRAISE* is genuine, you will most definitely 'feel' the presence of Holy Spirit – and the presence of God can't help but touch (and heal) your emotions. *PRAISE* & worship is not just something you do during Sunday morning church service. You want to live a life that's pleasing to God. The integrity of your life should be beautifully woven into the fabric of *PRAISE,* adoration, thanksgiving and worship to our Heavenly Father.

Composer Richard Smallwood wrote one of the most beautiful sacred songs in existence…

CENTER OF MY JOY

"Jesus, you're the center of my joy

All that's good and perfect comes from you

You're the joy of my contentment, hope for all I do

Jesus, you're the center of my joy" (Chorus)

It's always good to keep a *PRAISE* on your lips…it pleases the Father and keeps joy in your heart. It's hard to allow distractions and disappointments to overwhelm you when you focus on the Lord through the vehicle of *PRAISE!*

ISLE 8
ENTANGLEMENTS

"Stand fast therefore in the liberty wherewith Christ hath made us free, and be not entangled again with the yoke of bondage." Galatians 5:1

"For I know the thoughts that I think toward you, saith the Lord, thoughts of peace, and not of evil, to give you an expected end." Jeremiah 29:11

"Thou wilt keep him in perfect peace, whose mind is stayed on thee: because he trusteth in thee." Isaiah 26:3

Entanglements. Avoid them. You are good and grown now, you know the red flags...you really do. And in the case of late-bloomers, the red flags will still appear...it just may take you a little longer to recognize them.

In an effort to *be*, you ultimately allow what should never be. And if per chance you are that late-bloomer and you really didn't know, trust and believe, someone in your life was probably telling you, but were you listening? (Remember the Maya's?)

Entanglements come in all types, shapes and sizes, and although sometimes it could be, the entanglement may not always be that of the opposite sex. You can find yourself entangled with unscrupulous business partners, scams, wasting money, bad business deals, making rash decisions and the like…all in an effort to find, *you*. Trying to find your way. Trying to become whole again. After all, isn't that what the definition of being 'single' is? To be whole and complete. The writer of James in Chapter 1 verse 4 (KJV) reminds us; *"But let patience have her perfect work, that you may be perfect and entire, wanting nothing."*

My grandmother (We affectionately called her "Mama Walker") would say, *"Little girl, don't be in such a **hurry**!"* I really do understand, *"It sounds great!"*, *"He's is the one!"*, *"But he's SO FINE!!!"*, *"This business plan HAS to work!"* you tell yourself. You spend precious time convincing yourself that what you jumped into is the vehicle that will ultimately take you where you want to be. Alas, you jumped too quickly and you suffered a heart-break, lost hard-earned money, and wasted precious, valuable time. But please don't beat yourself up, that's the worst thing you could do. Accept it and move on. Journal your thoughts. Speak well of yourself. Learn from your mistakes, cry, repent (and mean it), pick your pretty self up and keep right on living.

"Do the best you can until you know better. Then when you know better, do better." -Maya Angelou

Learn how to wait on God. Quiet yourself and learn to hear His voice. Never, ever move in a season of desperation or out of fear. Allow faith to calmly walk you through to the Godly destination that your loving Heavenly Father has planned for you. Allow yourself to be put on the Potter's wheel and be made another, again, anew.

(3) "Then I went down to the potter's house, and, behold, he wrought a work on the wheels. (4) And the vessel that he made of clay was marred in the hand of the potter: so he made it again another vessel, as

41

seemed good to the potter to make it. (5) Then the word of the Lord came to me, saying, (6) O house of Israel, cannot I do with you as this potter? saith the Lord. Behold, as the clay is in the potter's hand, so are ye in mine hand, O house of Israel."
Jeremiah 18: 3-6

Quiet yourself before the Lord and allow Him to refresh and renew your spirit.

"But the God of all grace, who hath called us unto his eternal glory by Christ Jesus, after that ye have suffered a while, make you perfect, stablish, strengthen, settle you." I Peter 5:10

God will begin to block future entanglements (if you pay attention) and bring you to a place of peace that only He can provide.

ISLE 9
SINGLE DOESN'T MEAN ALONE

"Let your conversation be without covetousness; and be content with such things as ye have: for he hath said, I will never leave thee, nor forsake thee." Hebrews 13:5

"Peace I leave with you, my peace I give unto you: not as the world giveth, give I unto you. Let not your heart be troubled, neither let it be afraid." John 14:27

"Don't be afraid, for I am with you. Don't be discouraged, for I am your God. I will strengthen you and help you. I will hold you up with my victorious right hand." Isaiah 41:10 (NLT)

"Casting all your care upon him; for he careth for you" I Peter 5:7

You're not alone. I feel I must spend more time here due to the fact that so many 'unattached' women seem to be so desperately looking to be 'attached'…and the sooner, the better.

I want to share with you a few songs, two in particular (#1 & #2) with completely different messages. It may take a little time, but I hope you'll read all of the lyrics to the songs I've listed. I'm a very musical person, so I hope you will indulge me. What you allow yourself to listen to and absorb into your spirit, especially during times of loneliness and emotional pain can either be very uplifting or take you to the Isle of Major Depression.

(Example #1- a song that builds hope)

THE PROMISE

I'll never leave you,
Nether forsake you
No matter what you're going through
I have good plans for you
I'll be with you always

I'll never leave you,
Nether forsake you
No matter what you're going through

I have good plans for you
I'll be with you always

And when sorrow comes
And there's no other place to run
Just look to me and I'll be there
Just a whisper of a prayer

I'll be with you always
I'll never leave you,
Nether forsake you
No matter what you're going through
I have good plans for you
I'll be with you always
In stormy weather, it is my pleasure
I want to take care of all your needs
Trust me and you'll see
I'll be with you, always
-The late Pastor Andrae' Crouch

(Example #2- a song that questions hope)

ALONE AGAIN

In a little while from now
If I'm not feeling any less sour
I promise to treat myself

And visit a nearby tower
And climbing to the top
Will throw myself off
In an effort to
Make it clear to whoever
Wants to know what it's like when you're shattered

Left standing in the lurch at a church
Were people saying, My God, that's tough
She stood him up
No point in us remaining
We may as well go home
As I did on my own
Alone again, naturally
To think that only yesterday

I was cheerful, bright and gay
Looking forward to who wouldn't do
The role I was about to play
But as if to knock me down
Reality came around
And without so much as a mere touch
Cut me into little pieces
Leaving me to doubt
Talk about, God in His mercy

Oh, if he really does exist
Why did he desert me
In my hour of need

I truly am indeed
Alone again, naturally
It seems to me that
There are more hearts broken in the world
That can't be mended

Left unattended
What do we do
What do we do
Alone again, naturally
Looking back over the years
And whatever else that appears
I remember I cried when my father died
Never wishing to hide the tears

And at sixty-five years old
My mother, God rest her soul
Couldn't understand why the only man
She had ever loved had been taken
Leaving her to start
With a heart so badly broken
Despite encouragement from me
No words were ever spoken
And when she passed away
I cried and cried all day
Alone again, naturally
Alone again, naturally

-Gilbert O'Sullivan

Alone Again lyrics c Sony/ATV Music Publishing
LLC

Ladies! Please, please, please don't hurl
yourself (naturally or emotionally) off the top
of a building over a pair of pants! Over Breath
& Britches! (Old school will get that.)

Certainly not meaning to make light of this
subject, but *NO ONE* is worth you losing
your sanity over, and certainly not your life. If
you listen to too many of these heart-
wrenching, hopeless songs, you could find
yourself in a manic-depressive state of
mind....*over a man!* (*I wish I would!!!*)

Seriously, the best thing you can do for
yourself, is just to be yourself, keep living and
enjoy your life. Be creative and do what you
love! Create multiple success in your life! Be
excited about YOU and about your future!

I personally believe that there are some really
good men out there, looking for some really
good women. You want to be with someone
who really loves you, appreciates you, is
supportive and allows you to just 'be'. You

should be able to express yourself in ways that are pleasing to you, and that he appreciates.

We've heard it time and time again, if a man really wants a certain women, he will try to move heaven and earth to be with her.

The late Donny Hathaway was a beast; a musical genius. His songs are so heartfelt...

(Example #3 – The song every single woman wants to hear sung to her.)

<u>A SONG FOR YOU</u>

"I love you in a place where there's no space or time.
I love you for my life, you're a friend of mine
And when my life is over
Remember when we were together
We were alone and I was singing this song to you."

Performed by the incomparable,
the late Donny Hathaway (1971)
Lyrics originally by Leon Russell (1970)

(Example #4 – The heart of a man.)

<u>WHEN A MAN LOVES A WOMAN</u>
(Originally Performed by Percy Sledge)

When a man loves a woman
Can't keep his mind on nothing else
He'll trade the world
For the good thing he's found
If she's bad he can't see it
She can do no wrong
Turn his back on his best friend
If he put her down

When a man loves a woman
Spend his very last dime
Trying to hold on to what he needs
He'd give up all his comfort
Sleep out in the rain
If she said that's the way it ought to be

Well, this man loves a woman
I gave you everything I had
Trying to hold on to your precious love
Baby, please don't treat me bad

When a man loves a woman
Down deep in his soul
She can bring him such misery
If she plays him for a fool
He's the last one to know
Loving eyes can't ever see

When a man loves a woman

He can do no wrong
He can never own some other girl
Yes when a man loves a woman
I know exactly how he feels
'Cause baby, baby, baby, you're my world
When a man loves a woman

Songwriters
ANDREW JAMES WRIGHT,
CALVIN HOUSTON LEWIS
Published by
Lyrics c Sony/ATV Music publishing LLC,
Warner/Chappell Music, Inc.
Song Discussions is protected by U.S. Patent 9401941.
Other patents pending

And a portion of a little something from my own heart....

<u>I WONDER WHAT IT FEELS LIKE</u>

I wonder what it feels like to be loved
I wonder what it feels like to be held by
the one who loves me
I wonder what it feels like to be truly loved
By the one, the only one

-DaLoria Mondesir ©2014

Please know your worth. Always remember that you are a daughter of the King.

Okay, some of you may be saying, *"Don't over spiritualize it."* *"I'm tired of sleeping with my pillows!"* Trust me, I hear you but that's where know your worth comes in the most. Simply put, love and value yourself enough to stay faithful to the Lord.

I think the "Don't Settle" topic has been thoroughly beat to death, but for some reason unknown to me, some of us are still doing it. It's not worth it to be with someone that's not good for you just to say that you have a man. (But in reality, do you really have him? Just a thought.)

Longing to be in a healthy, Godly relationship is honorable. I would humbly suggest that you don't spend every waking hour thinking about being part of a couple. Just allow God to work on you, and you do what's necessary to work on yourself. For all you know, the Lord could be preparing that special man just for you right now, but please be healed and whole before you enter into the next relationship.

It's important to have a good balance of

staying busy, quiet time, exercise, mini-travel trips, concerts, etc. Do things that you enjoy doing…even spending time alone and getting re-acquainted with YOU.

This Isle of Singleness is actually a gift. I often find myself at my bedside or on the floor praying at very odd hours in the middle of the night. My relationship with the Lord is the most important thing in my life. I love Him, and endeavor to serve Him with all that I am…and I willingly serve Him. I belong to the Lord and my life is not my own….and that's a beautiful thing. I cherish the love of my Savior, and I want to live a life that's pleasing to Him. He died on the cross for me and for you. I can do nothing less than give Him my life in return.

ISLE 10
THE TWO "C'S
COFFEE & CONFIDENCE!

"Being confident of this very thing, that he which hath begun a good work in you will perform it until the day of Jesus Christ:" Philippians 1:6

"And blessed is she that believed: for there shall be a performance of those things which were told her from the Lord." St. Luke 1:45

"I have coffee in one hand and confidence in the other!" Evangelist Joyce L. Rodgers, TWITTER, August 18, 2017

The two "C's" sound like, *"God's got this!" Get up! Let's go!"*

For me, there something almost euphoric

about smelling freshly brewed coffee in my kitchen! It excites me and comforts me all at the same time. I also love going into coffee shops sometimes for the sheer pleasure of being there surrounded by varied aromas of rich, delicious coffee!! (I think I'm addicted!! LOL!!) It's like confidence-in-a-cup kinda' thing. It's like seeing an;

Anointed, Attractive, Attentive, Adventurous,
Blessed, Built, Business-Minded,
Caring, Committed, Comical, Consoling,
Compassionate, Common Sensed,
Determined, Distinguished, Dedicated,
Educated, Established, Entrepreneurial,
Empathetic, Exciting,
Faithful, Funny, Fit, Fabulous,
Financially- Secure, Fine,
Genuine, Gorgeous, Gifted, Grateful, Giver,
Great Communicator,
Honest, Handsome, Happy, Healthy,
Helpful, Healed,
Intelligent, Integral, Inspired,
Jovial, Jolly,
Kindhearted, Kinglike, Knowledgeable, Keen,
Loyal, Loving, Leader, Level-Headed,

Life-Partner,
Mature, Manly, Ministry-Minded,
Marriage-Minded, Motivated, Musical,
No-nonsense, Nice, Noble,
Optimistic, Out-Going,
Peaceful, Polite, Positive, Pro-Active,
Purposeful, Personable,
Qualified (by God),
Reasonable, Ready, Respectful,
Saved, Submitted to God, Sexy, Smart,
Sincere, Sensitive, Strong, Smiling,
(Single-of course!)
Talented, Thoughtful, Thinker,
Unique, Unafraid, Understanding,
Victorious, Vigilant, Visionary, Valiant,
Witty, Well-spoken, Well-Adjusted,
Wealthy,
Xenodochial (Yes, I found "X"!!!)
Zestful…
…BLACK MAN!

(OK, gimme a break!!! I started thinking about how valuable black men are, and this is where my mind went!!! I had to cover everything from A-Z!!! Ya' gotta' love me! LOL!!! No offense to other colors and cultures, I just personally prefer my man to be "Venti Dark

Roast"– like my coffee; with a little cream & and a whole lot of sweetness!! LOL!!) Have mercy! LOL!! *(Aww, loosen up! This is funny – and you know it!!)*

Know who you are and walk in it. You are a daughter of the Most High! Your presence should command the room when you arrive.

By the way ladies, I've been told that there is nothing more attractive to a man then a woman that operates in confidence. *(BTW, shhhh, don't mention this to anyone, but if we expect the man to have all of this and more, we should be bringing a little 'something-something' to the table as well. Don't you agree? Sigh & Selah)*

ISLE 11
PLEASE DON'T KILL YOUR FRIENDS!

"A friend loveth at all times, and a brother is born for adversity." Proverbs 17:17

"The Lord will perfect that which concerns me; Your mercy, O Lord, endures forever; Do not forsake the works of Your hands." Psalm 138:8

"For the LORD is good; his mercy is everlasting; and his truth endureth to all generations." Psalm 100:5

Ok, it happened. There was a breakup. It hurt. All you know is that right now you need to talk to somebody!!! Anybody!!!

There's your truth, his truth, but ultimately, there's God's truth and His truth is really the only truth that matters. Others always seem to have 'their' truth about your (past)

58

relationships as well – even from the outside looking in, a lot of the time, they're clueless. And other people's opinions are just that. Opinions. People are however, entitled to think and say whatever they'd like, and it's their prerogative to do so. It's also your prerogative to listen (or not) and accept or reject what's been told you.

The Bible teaches us to seek out *wisdom* and *counsel*, and I'm all for it! However, I would caution you about seeking too many 'opinions' from the 'squad', or outer-circle if you will. It can be too much. As many different people as you ask, there will more than likely be as many different opinions for you to absorb and digest. It can be overwhelming trying to sort through all of the varied opinions. After all, they are all your 'friends' and they have your best interest at heart. Right? Not always. There's your inner-circle friends and outer-circle acquaintances.

Know your 'squad'...some may need to be moved from your inner circle of a few close and trusted friends, to the outer-circle of acquaintances. The people you 'hang with' are a reflection of you, so choose your friends wisely. Also, everyone can't speak into your life, nor can you always depend on your outer-circle for answers to your relationship problems.

Real friends, real sisters come in small numbers, but that's really all you need. Too much of a thing, is just that...too much! Even *"Too much of a good thing, is still too much!"* (Mr. Napoleon Hill – "Think and Grow Rich") It can and will sometimes confuse you and God is not the author of confusion.

Just my personal choice, but I'm very cautious about entering into Online Dating Relationship Support Groups, Group Coaching and Counseling and alike. Although I'm a huge fan of professional private counseling, I personally don't relish entering ongoing conversations with complete strangers sharing my private experiences with them, and also trusting them to keep my business private/within the group...it just doesn't sound like a good idea to me. I'm not a counselor, and neither are most of these people.

You can hear so many varied opinions, and it can be confusing and just way too much. You may already be in a situation that requires healing, or are in the process of healing. This I feel, has the potential of creating more damage and seemingly can add to your already painful and sensitive state of mind…especially if it's not biblically based counseling/advice.

It's like constantly and consistently watching a particular Soap Opera, the drama never ends. Ultimately, you may still be 'sick' and the overabundance of listening to everyone else's woes, has the potential of emotionally damaging you. Even listening to their relationship successes can be depressing if you aren't currently dating anyone.

If you have an open sore, you certainly don't pour alcohol on it, and then apply a number of different medications on top of it along with DIY treatment to promote healing. You more than likely choose one method, and use it consistently until healing takes place. It's like going to a buffet, it's impossible (for most) to eat everything served…it's simply too much.

Absolutely no offense meant to those that facilitate groups of this nature, or to those that have chosen this route for their personal healing, but as I stated before, that's my choice…I'm personally not cool with it. Find what works for you. Pray and ask God for direction.

I'm a huge fan of Author and Speaker, Pastor Michelle McKinney Hammond. Her books and messages on YouTube have played a pivotal role in my healing process during a time when I felt like I wasn't going to make it. If I'm ever afforded the opportunity to meet her personally, I would love to thank her for the transparency she has demonstrated in ministry and books. I've been told that the pain and trouble we go through isn't always for us, but when we come out victoriously, we are then in a position to help someone else make it through.

(Seek wise, seasoned, personal and

professional counsel if you can. You'll know it's wise if what you're hearing is based on the word of God.)

Now, about the statement I made earlier, you want to talk to someone, anyone. You know you can always talk to your closest friends, and although they love you and want to help, it's not fair to overload them with your relationship problems. There is a fine-balancing line, it's certainly fine to talk to your friends, just don't kill your relationships by always singing a "Woe Is Me" song. When you hear them gently directing the conversation elsewhere, follow their lead. There's usually a reason for it.

You'll know those that are the true sista-friends. I must say, I love my beautiful sista-friends! Their personalities are so varied it's amazing, yet they all have a common lineage. They love God, are intelligent, beautiful, talented….and they just happen to care about me. I've given my sista-friends 'titles' based on how God has gifted them in helping me through my 'crazy'. There's…

Sista Sharon-The Intercessor
Sista Francelia – The Revelator
Sista Colleen – The Common-Sense Queen
Sista Floetta- The Insightful One
Sista Kiki – The Real Deal
Sista Deborah – The Truth Teller
Sista Narda – The Welcoming One
Sista Honey – The Big Sister
Sista Betty – The Prayer Warrior
Sista Debbie - The Listening Ear
Sista Chari – The Loving Encourager
And my special 'Old Friend' - The Nurturer.

This list would not be complete without mentioning one of my dearest Sista-Friend's that's gone home to be with the Lord, Sista Merlinda – The Concerned One. I miss her dearly. I'll see you in the morning, sis.

(Notice, not one of them is a Fixer.) They don't try to fix my problems for me, and neither do they purposely say things to hurt me, but rather to help….but sometimes receiving help, may hurt…for the moment.

A true sista-girlfriend will never try to set you up for a fall. They will tell you the truth because they love you. And in return for them listening to your rants and fits, because they are tried, true and trusted sista-friends *and you love them*, you'll listen. (I know I'm in trouble now…I started calling names, please forgive me.)

It's important to have some platonic friendships with Godly men as well….you get to hear how the "other side" thinks. That's important. (Ok guys, if you happen to be reading this book, you know who you are, thank you!)

And here's my opinion on "unwelcome, negative opinions". Table them. Seek the face of God. Tell Him what concerns you. Go to the Word of God and see what He says about the situation and HIS WORD is really the only word that matters. Don't allow other (negative) people's "truth" to become your 'truth', or their "story" your story; neither allow anyone to project their fears or relationship experiences onto you.

And there's usually that one real hurt woman that claims that all men are Dogs…but yet and still, she wants to be in a relationship.

(Wouldn't that mean that she's ultimately going to end up with a "Dog"? You can tell her, "Buh-bye, now." She's not good for you.)

Remember who you are…that you are fearfully and wonderfully made. Know that. Walk in it. Own it.

ISLE 12
THE KITCHEN TABLE

"In the multitude of my thoughts within me thy comforts delight my soul" Psalms 94:19

"It is the Lord who goes before you; He will be with you. He will not fail you or abandon you. Do not fear or be dismayed." Deuteronomy 31:8

"I'm just someone who likes cooking and for whom sharing food is a form of expression." -Maya Angelou

I love going to visit my 'Old Friend'. Her place of abode has a very comfortable and welcoming 'At Home' feel to it. It's peaceful and serene. She's a wonderful cook and her kitchen is always filled with wonderful aromas. I could sit at her kitchen table for hours just for the peace alone. Her coffee blends are smooth, soothing and delicious. I appreciate that she always has that special coffee creamer that I love when I arrive. She goes through the trouble of preparing varied and unique appetizers for everyone in the house. Even though we'd lost contact for a while, she's been a true friend from day one.

Recently, I was on the phone speaking with my 'Old Friend'; the Nurturer, and she mentioned the subject of making sure that as a single person, that I actually ate right – that I nourished myself properly. Am I devaluing myself by not always treating myself nutritionally well? Are you? (Thank you, Dr. Beryl New!).

This was a difficult Isle to write about, because it's always been a struggle. I don't necessarily overeat, my problem is eating the wrong things at the wrong times. Comfort food has its place, but emotional eating should be monitored. (I'm preaching to the choir here.)

At my Old Friend's house growing up, her mother's Kitchen Table was a gathering place for friends, old and new. Many candid girl-talks and a lot of laughter happened while eating homemade tacos at that Kitchen Table. Sadly, her mother is no longer with us and is dearly missed. Her welcoming spirit, candid conversations about life, and Kitchen Table legacy has been passed on to my precious Old Friend, and I'm grateful.

I don't know about you, but as a busy and involved, working *Single Again* women, I tend to fill up my life so much that most of the time, that I don't always take the necessary amount of time to properly nurture myself. I can sometimes go from morning till night, on only one meal…if that. I'm very guilty of just grabbing some fast-food or snacks on the way to my next 'thing-to-do'. I do cook from time to time, but it seems that I'm not home much to actually eat what I've prepared, or I'm just simply too tired to eat when I arrive home and I completely bypass the kitchen and go straight to bed. This is my rough spot, and I endeavor to do better.

My own mother would say things like, *"You've got to treat yourself better than that!"* or, *"Did you take your vitamins today? They are not doing you any good sitting in the bottle."* As I write this Devotional, my own dear mother is suffering from Dementia and can no longer talk to me. I can talk to her, and I do. I tell her everything. I'm so grateful for the lessons she's taught me, and I will forever be in her loving debt…..and I wish I'd listened a little closer to her wisdom. Mrs. Artie Mae Walker Smith, a.k.a. "Queen Bee" – *loving you is like food to my soul.* (Boyz-To-Men, thank you.)

The Kitchen Table reference reminds me that maybe we all need to slow down just a bit, and enjoy our surroundings, feed and nourish our minds, body's and souls with the good things that we all need and desire. It doesn't hurt to bless our sisters with the comfort of a good cup of coffee, a listening ear, good conversation and real friendship. I don't mean to lecture right here, but it's just a reminder to us all to treat ourselves and our sista's well.

ISLE 13
LIPSTICK ON THE MIRROR

"Who can find a virtuous woman? For her price is far above rubies." Proverbs 31:10

"I will praise thee; for I am fearfully and wonderfully made: marvelous are thy works; and that my soul knoweth right well." Psalm 141:14

I met an amazing woman on a particular day. We'd seen each other before at different Jurisdictional and National church functions, yet we'd never really had an opportunity to meet or visit. During the course of my work day, I had reason to visit the office where she works.

As I was taken into her office to be introduced, we made eye contact and the "Sista-Smiles" and "Quiet Screams" ensued! As I approached her desk, she, with erect posture so confidently looked directly at me and began to eloquently quote a portion of a speech given by former President Nelson Mandela;

"Our Deepest Fear"

Our deepest fear is not that we are inadequate. Our deepest fear is that we are powerful beyond measure. It is our light, not our darkness, that most frightens us. We ask ourselves, who am I to be brilliant, gorgeous, talented and fabulous?

Actually, who are you not to be?

You are a child of God. Your playing small doesn't serve the world. There's nothing enlightened about shrinking so that other people won't feel insecure around you.

We were born to manifest the glory of God that is within us. It's not just in some of us; it's in everyone. And as we let our own light shine, we unconsciously give other people permission to do the same. As we are liberated from our own fears, our presence automatically liberates others.

President Nelson Mandela -1994 Inaugural

I was quickly embarrassed because I didn't

recognize that these words were that of former President Mandela. She promptly Googled the speech and later sent it to me via text message that read, "Your new travel Companion for 30 days!" Wow!

This awesome woman of God for a season of time, would constantly encourage me and would send me 'assignments' via text messages. I believe the most powerful assignment she sent me, (and for some reason the most difficult) was for me to write on my bathroom mirror in lipstick, *"I AM ENOUGH"*.

Reading it every day was sometimes (most times) very challenging. Well, it wasn't so much reading it, as it was trying to convince myself to actually believe these coral colored words on my bathroom mirror. You know how it is. People often assume that if you 'look' okay, you must 'be' okay. So up until that point, I'd found a way to make it through the day. I'd already believed that I was lacking in a number of areas, so reading the Lipstick Letters was very difficult to say the least.

Moment of transparency: Often I would find myself standing in front of the mirror – forced to, if you will because I had to 'put my face on' and get ready to go out and function normally in public. I couldn't forget to use my eye cream at night and my under-eye concealer in the morning to camouflage the puffiness from once again crying myself to sleep the night before. It was depression. I'd given my power away. This seemingly strong woman of God was in a bona-fide state of depression. Overweight, and out-of-shape, and not feeling particularly attractive, I felt as if no one would ever truly love me.

Over time it's amazing what happened! I kept reading the Lipstick Letters, sometimes multiple times a day and guess what? I actually begin to believe what I was reading. I was absorbing this awesome and truth-filled fact about myself! I was finally coming to a place where I could regain my power. I finally believed that *I AM ENOUGH!! AND YOU ARE TOO!!*

The amazing thing during all of this was that

this woman and I really didn't know each other. She didn't know my story, and I didn't know hers. As far as I knew, she didn't know anything about me…at all…so why would she give me such an arduous task! Because God will place the right person in your life at the right time to assist in nourishing and feeding the emotions of your soul. It's required. It's necessary and everybody needs a 'Janice' in their life. These prophetic messengers and intercessors are sent from the Lord just when you need encouragement the most…they don't offer their opinion, they give you solid, proven words that heal. No need to seek them out, but do be aware when they show up in your life. Ms. Janice Smallwood McKinzie, *Thank You!*

I challenge you ladies, to the same task that the lovely Janice assigned to me. In big, bold lipstick letters, adorn your bathroom mirror with…***I AM ENOUGH!***

YOU HAVE NOTHING TO LOSE AND EVERYTHING TO GAIN!

ISLE 14
THE QUEEN SITS

"She is clothed with strength and dignity, she laughs without fear of the future." Proverbs 31:25

"I do not want a husband who honours me as a queen, if he does not love me a woman." Elizabeth I

Have you ever noticed that while royalty is seated, those in her service are moving about in their assigned tasks? They know both their position and job well. The Queen need not speak or instruct except when she chooses to do so. She can peacefully sit without (outward) anxiety, knowing that all functions in her 'Kingdom' and those in servitude to her will function like clock-work.

My point, NEVER chase after a man. If he wants you, he knows how and where to find you. He also knows full well what to do and he'll make the joyful effort to come and get you.

You have an assurance and know, and possibly at times remind yourself that you are royalty because you are a daughter of the King. God knew you before the foundation of the world, and fashioned you in His image and in His likeness. He created and formed you into the beauty that you are. Jesus loves you like no other and His love never fails.

It doesn't take any money at all to treat yourself like the queen that you are. It's your mindset. It's how you talk to yourself. It's how you treat yourself. Yes, you can take yourself out on a date…spend a little cash, and enjoy yourself…and you should most definitely do that! You should spoil and treat yourself once in a while to the spa or beautiful bouquet of your favorite fragrant flowers….you should most definitely do that as well!!! However, the best thing you can do for yourself is to speak well of yourself, to yourself.

When you go to the Manufacture of YOU (a term adapted from the late Dr. Myles Monroe), He will tell you that you are fearfully and wonderfully made! That He made you in His own image! You are the apple of His eye!

Girl, please! Do you know who you are??? When you really know, you will then realize and accept **Whose** you are, it will be so much easier to understand **who** YOU are. You are so special to the Creator the hairs on your head are numbered!! Not the number of strands of hair on your head mind you, but each individual strand of hair has been assigned its own number!! (Strand #43,564 just got caught in the hairbrush!) How cool is that?

(6) *"What is the price of five sparrows-two copper coins? Yet God does not forget a single one of them."*
(7)*"And the very hairs on your head are all numbered. So don't be afraid; you are more valuable to God than a whole flock of sparrows"* Luke 12:6-7

Take the time to examine your own uniqueness! Your God-Given talents and abilities! Love yourself! Get in the mirror and tell yourself every good and wonderful thing that God has said about you! (Thank you, Dr. Barbara McCoo Lewis!)

Embrace your beauty, your uniqueness, everything about you that makes you, YOU! YOU are beautiful! YOU are awesome! YOU are creative! YOU are amazing! YOU are brilliant! YOU are smart! YOU are capable! YOU are the handiwork of the Creator.

ISLE 15
WHO'S IN YOUR EAR?

"So then faith cometh by hearing, and hearing by the word of God." Romans 10:17

"You don't let go of a bad relationship because you stop caring about them. You let go because you finally start caring about you." -Charles Orlando

I believe there is most certainly a song to fit every occasion, both secular and sacred. We don't talk much about secular songs in church, but once in a while I enjoy listening to some *quality* old school – like The Spinners, The Temptations, and of course the incomparable Mr. Stevland Hardaway Judkins a.k.a. Mr. Stevie Wonder! Ladies, whether or not we want to admit it, some of those songs showed us the heart of a man in love with one very special woman. The Emotions, Ms. Lalah Hathaway, Ms. Anita Baker and the late Ms. Natalie Cole among others, have also sung some very beautiful ballads about lost loves as well, or the love that we hope and pray will someday be.

I believe it's a very natural thing to want to hear songs that bring comfort to our broken heart. Music also connects us, and certain songs let us know that we are not the only woman (or man) that have dealt with a break-up and heartbreak.

It's so beneficial spending your free time listening to those things that will build you up. Read the Bible and literature that will strengthen and encourage you. Purposely listen to those positive voices in your life that you know love you and want nothing more than to build you up. Listen to those sistas that are interceding for you.

There are certain Pastors and Evangelists that I listen to online on a regular basis. I enjoy doing so because it helps me stay centered and encouraged.

Please stay far away from drama-filled individuals and situations that will add to the pain that you may already be experiencing. Learn to enjoy spending time with yourself!

(After all, if you don't enjoy spending time with yourself, why would anyone else want to….just a thought.) If you haven't already done so, learn to love you – after all, you are pretty incredible!

Give yourself a break from social media sometimes. Not meaning to insult your intelligence, but of course you know that a lot of the 'selfies' taken, are taken repeatedly to get just the right angle and the 'right' filter used to present an image that will always present the subject in the best possible light.

There are a few people who post that want to make everyone believe that their life is *always* fun and exciting – no issues. It's simply not true. We *all* have some issues going on because it's just life. I'm not suggesting that people post everything about their life, but I do wonder about some singles (and even some couples) that constantly and consistently post where they are and what they are doing….sometimes they are just *doing too much*.

All in all, you must decide what and who you will allow to speak into your life. If you determine that the outcome of taking heed to certain individuals is hurting you and will hinder your healing process, then you may want to reconsider talking to and spending time with them. It's your choice.

FINAL THOUGHTS...

I pray that the words of this little Devotional have made a positive impact on your life for the furtherance of the Kingdom of God. Many of the transparent words written were done so in the wee hours of the night with tears in my eyes as certain personal past relationship 'events' that I'd seek to bury were made alive again in my memory. I knew, (as our Senior Saints would say) down in my *"Knower"* that I didn't go through all of the pain I've been through for nothing. I pray that the negative stigma of being 'single' has been positively reintroduced to you as that of one that is whole and not alone. I pray that you've been blessed, and encouraged to reach for everything that God has prepared for you. Know that there will most certainly be a battle, but more importantly know that the battle belongs to the Lord. (2 Chronicles 20:15).

"And for your shame, ye shall have DOUBLE; and for confusion they shall rejoice in their portion: therefore in their land they shall possess the DOUBLE: everlasting joy shall be unto them"

Isaiah 61:7

THANK YOU…

First to my Lord and Savior Jesus Christ, to God who gave His son Jesus to die on the cross at Calvary on our behalf, and to Holy Spirit who comforts me daily.

To my parents, the late Deacon Alton C. Smith, Sr. and my beloved mother Evangelist Missionary Artie M. Smith. Without both of you, there would be no 'me'! (Smile) I love you from the bottom of my heart!

To my children – I love you more than life itself. Without each of you, I would have never discovered and experienced the joy of giving birth, nor of bringing precious and unique lives into this world. I've had the distinct pleasure of watching you grow into your awesome adulthood. Your presence and impact you have made on this world is monumental. You are the beats of my heart!

To my first (and at this point) only grandson, you make my heart sing! Nana loves you!!!

To my "Old Friend" – The Nurturer. Thank you for reading every word and assisting me with your keen sense of editing. You literally read, EVERY. SINGLE. WORD! (*inside*)

To Professor Sandra Lassiter. You have always encouraged me to sing for His glory, to study to show myself approved, to build, and to do my best for the Lord and the Kingdom of God.

To my new friend and Literary Consultant Dr. Beryl New. You have from day one counseled me in this project, reignited my vision that I tried so desperately to suppress, and spoken words of life that have quickly brought this project to manifestation.

To Dr. Barbara McCoo Lewis, International General Supervisor | Jurisdictional Supervisor of Southern California First Ecclesiastical Jurisdiction Church of God and Christ - **and my spiritual mom**. Thank you for praying for me and pushing me to excellence. You believed in me when I didn't believe in myself. I will always be grateful.

To my Pastor, Superintendent Jeffrey M. Lewis, Sr. Thank you for consistently preaching and teaching the pure Word of God. You have taught us to stand for holiness and righteousness with conviction and no compromise.

To Lady Floetta Lewis, thank you for being a beautiful example of a woman that's loved unconditionally.

ABOUT THE AUTHOR...

DaLoria (Smith) Mondesir is originally from Altadena, California. A *Single Again* woman, a '60's baby, mother of three beautifully spirited and dynamic souls, and a grandmother of one gorgeous grandson ....and waiting for more! (Smile)

DaLoria simply a woman forgiven and made whole by the love of Jesus Christ. She endeavors to continuously seek His face, and serve Him with her entire being! She serves as the Executive Administrative Assistant (Daily Operations) to the General Supervisor, Dr. Barbara McCoo Lewis, International Department of Women, Church of God in Christ, Inc. DaLoria currently resides in Southern California and is an active and faithful member of the Church of God in Christ.

AUTHOR'S NOTE...

This little Devotional was literally 'downloaded' into my spirit beginning Saturday, August 12, 2017. The bulk of the writing with the exception of one additional 'Isle' (that I struggled to include) and final edits, was completed on Wednesday, September 21, 2017, the beginning of Rosh Hashanah – the Jewish New Year. The writing of this Devotional in its entirety was completed on Saturday, September 30, 2017. The dates are I believe significant because the birthing of this book coincides with the Jewish New Year 5778, which represents divine completeness (9). The oil flowed and God allowed me to finish this book in record time.

Producing and publishing anything to do with the transparency of being *Single Again* was never planned or even imagined prior to this time.

I'm so grateful to the Lord for entrusting me with this assignment. This has truly been a God-inspired, labor of love and the birthing of a new chapter in my life….and excitedly, there's more to come!

Plans for additional *Single Again – The Devotional* volumes are already in the outlined stages. Upon publication of this Devotional, I will begin work on the accompanying *Single Again – The Journal.*

When it becomes available, I would encourage you to pour out your heart on the pages of the *Single Again* journal designed especially for YOU! Journaling will help you sift through your own private, painful and joyful emotions. After some time, I would suggest you go back and read your own journaling. When you've decided to take a step forward to your own emotional freedom, you will find the beautiful, talented and "fabtabulous" YOU that's always been there.

Finally, thank you purchasing this Devotional and more importantly, investing in yourself. I encourage you to be silent before the Lord, listening for His voice and loving instruction. You never know what God has in store for you! *Shalom!*

You are invited to visit DaLoria Mondesir online at:

FaceBook – fb.me/daloriaonline (Send page messages at m.me/daloriaonline)

InstaGram - @SingleAgainTheDevotional

Twitter - @daloriaonline

LinkedIn -
www.linkedin.com/in/daloriaonline

On the web - www.DaloriaOnline.com

Email: info@daloriaonline.com

(At the time of this publishing, every effort has been made to provide correct and current online contact information. Please send all correspondence electronically to one of the online addresses listed above.)

Made in the USA
San Bernardino, CA
15 November 2017